P9-CCX-485

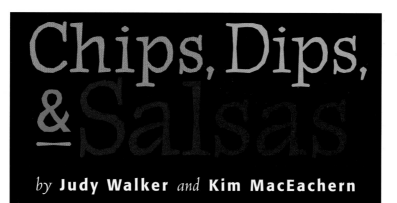

Chips, Dips, & Salsas

by **Judy Walker** *and* **Kim MacEachern**

photography by **Christopher Marchetti**

NORTHLAND PUBLISHING

With love to the Walkers:
Dave, Mack, Vera, Charlie,
and Beverly.
—J. W.

To my mother, Jacquie
Weedon, who took a dip
during the making of this
book, but is once again in
chipper health and back to her
old salsa style.
—K. M.

Copyright © 1999 by Judy Walker and Kim MacEachern
Photographs copyright © 1999 by Northland Publishing

All rights reserved.

This book may not be reproduced in whole or in part, by any means (with
the exception of short quotes for the purpose of review), without permission
of the publisher. For information, address Permissions, Northland Publishing
Company, P. O. Box 1389, Flagstaff, AZ 86002-1389.

www.northlandbooks.com

The text type was set in Weiss and Formata
The display type was set in Journal
Photographs by Christopher Marchetti

Composed in the United States of America
Printed in China

All cooking temperatures in this book refer to the Fahrenheit scale. The use
of trade names does not imply an endorsement by the product manufacturer.

FIRST IMPRESSION, August 1999

05   7   6   5

ISBN 13: 978-0-87358-737-2 (pb)
ISBN 10: 0-87358-737-5 (pb)

Library of Congress Cataloging-in-Publication Data

Walker , Judy Hille.
   Chips, dips, and salsas / by Judy Walker and Kim MacEachern.
      p.   cm.
   Includes index.
      1. Dips (Appetizers) 2. Salsas (Cookery)   I. MacEachern, Kim.
   II. Title.
   TX740.W236   1999
   641.8'12–dc21   99-17218

CONTENTS

ACKNOWLEDGMENTS

The authors want to thank Dave Jenney, Erin Murphy, Stephanie Bucholz, and all the folks at Northland Publishing for their idea and all the encouragement.

We are also deeply indebted to our recipe contributors. Without these wonderful people, you would be holding a much skinnier book! Thank you to Jacquie Weedon, Sharon Cooper, Kathy Blake-Novotny, Sarah Staley, Cherilee Churchill, Carol Buto, Joy Lambert, Mark Lauffer, Lupita Banuelos, Elaine Bell, Jan Trower, Mary Stutsman, Bev Walker, Mack Walker, and Anita Mabante Leach. Thanks also to our recipe tasters, who include Walt Weedon, Bill and Bobbie Trower, Cynthia Seelhammer, Tom Marcinko, Sally Stearman, Charlie Walker and Vera Walker. We salute your perceptive taste buds!

Thank you, also, to those who encouraged us in this project, including Michelle Anderson, Bill Eimers, Chauntelle Wilson, Teresa MacEachern, Lucile Trower, Winnie Grasselli, Jo Anne Izumi, Peter Van Dyke, and the food! team at The Arizona Republic.

Finally, the best for last: We could never have done this without the support, love and constructive commentary from Doug, Melanie, Dave, and Mack, our personal in-house consultants. Thank you!

Introduction

Welcome to our Southwestern world of chips, dips, and salsas. Salsas are staples of Mexican cultures that date back thousands of years. They're married to tortilla chips, another favorite from pre-Columbian times that are now more popular than ever. Dips came to popularity in the fifties, and continue to be staples at every entertaining occasion. ❦ Our definition of these three

now-classic snack items extends to include fruit salsas, hot sauces, layered spreads, nachos—even dessert salsas and dips. Salsa is such a dynamic condiment that it can be a relish for grilled fish or meats, an ingredient in more complex dishes, or a savory addition to stews, casseroles, or macaroni and cheese. ❦ Dips can go far beyond onion soup mix, too. Layered versions can star on any buffet. Realizing that nachos are sometimes a meal in many homes, we include new ideas for this ball-park favorite in the chip chapter. ❦ We've also included ways to make our recipes more healthful and fun, especially chips. You can bake instead of fry them, or cut them into cute shapes and use them as garnishes! You can substitute low-fat or non-fat dairy products for cream cheese, yogurt, mayonnaise, and sour cream with great results. ❦ Our philosophy is that recipes are not cast in stone. Add your own embellishments—your own style—to our suggested formulas. As the world shrinks, tradition takes on new meanings, new forms, new fusions. Let your imagination and your taste buds run wild as you explore the fresh and fruity, hot and savory, just plain tasty world of chips, dips, and salsas.

Previous page: Tuscan Salsa, page 53.

THE PANTRY

The mere thought of someone dropping by unexpectedly can strike terror into the stressed-out hearts of even the most practiced overachievers. But by keeping a few things on hand, you can be ready for the comfort of a fresh snack at any time. Keep chips in your cupboard and some onions and cheese around, and you're ready for any emergency. If you can grow a few herbs and pepper plants in your flower garden, you're miles ahead of the game.

Fresh is always fantastic, and you may be surprised to learn that the quality of today's canned foods is nutritionally superior to those of years past. Keep an eye on the canned foods in the supermarket for new flavor combinations. Here are our suggestions for the basic pantry collection that will allow you to whip up a dip or salsa on a moment's notice:

CANNED AND BOTTLED

Tomatoes: crushed, whole, and cut; Mexican-style with onions and chiles, such as Ro-tel brand; tomato paste; Mexican-style tomato sauce, such as El Pato brand

Beans: black, kidney, garbanzo, Great Northern, cannellini, charro

Soups: tomato, cream of shrimp, cream of chicken or celery

Vinegars: rice, cider, red wine, balsamic

Hot sauces such as Tabasco, Durkee's, and Louisiana Hot Sauce

Crushed pineapple

Mandarin oranges

Honey

Whole kernel corn

Roasted red bell peppers

Green chiles, diced and whole

Chipotle chiles in adobo sauce

Mole sauce

Pickled garlic

Baby shrimp

Chopped clams

Canned roast beef

Canned cooked chicken

DRIED AND PACKAGED

Sugars: granulated, confectioner's, brown

Sugar substitute

Basil

Cumin

Oregano

Garlic powder

Red chile flakes

Chili powder

Cayenne pepper

Dried onion soup mix

Pasteurized processed cheese, with and without chiles

PEPPERS: MINI-GLOSSARY OF OUR FAVORITES

Anaheim: Mild, all-purpose long green chile, best when roasted. Often used for rellenos.

Jalapeño: Another good-for-everything chile, hotter and shorter than the Anaheim. Great stuffed with peanut butter!

Chipotles: Smoked jalapeños that can be found dried (they keep forever) or canned in adobo sauce. Canned chipotles are easier to locate; check Mexican or Southwestern catalogs for dried chipotles.

Poblano: Large, dark green chile with broad shoulders. Excellent flavor, not as hot as a jalapeño, not as mild as an Anaheim. Also terrific when roasted.

Habanero: The hottest pepper, sometimes called a Chinese lantern. Know your audience when serving habaneros! A little goes a very long way.

Serrano: About as hot as a jalapeño, small, slender, green.

Tepín, pequin, and chiltepin chiles: Tiny, round, or pointed chiles. Quite hot, almost always found dried. All are related and some even grow wild in the Southwest. Crush the dried form when using.

For convenience, we have classified the recipes according to an important aspect of each dish.

Look for this box: | Make Ahead |

Though most are self-explanatory, a few may need elaboration:

Almost a Meal: More substantial than an appetizer.

Chafing Dish: Serve in a chafing dish, slow cooker, or fondue pot (or any dish with a heat source).

Festive: Fun to make and eat.

Have on Hand: Ingredients are easy to keep on hand for unexpected cravings.

Make Ahead: Keeps well and can be prepared in advance.

Muy Picante: Very hot.

Chips

Making your own chips is a wonderful thing to do for parties. Plan to make only as many as you will use for that meal or event. They are delicious hot, so if you can make them just before or as your guests arrive, so much the better. Our advice is to make them no more than two hours before you plan to

serve them. Unlike commercial chips, they will not stay crisp for very long and it's difficult to reheat them satisfactorily. ✌ You can make chips significantly lower in fat by baking them, which is very easy to do. Or you can take the traditional route and deep-fry them. ✌ Here's an idea: Make sweet chips as well as savory ones! Baked flour tortilla chips seasoned with cinnamon-sugar can be used to accompany any fruit salsa, or to garnish desserts such as flan or an otherwise ho-hum scoop of ice cream or frozen yogurt. Flavored flour tortillas sold for "wraps" make great chips as well. ✌ It's easy to stack tortillas and cut them into wedges with a knife or kitchen shears. Or, if you've got those shears in your hand and you feel creative, you can cut tortillas into sunbursts, moons, stars, letters—whatever—to decorate dips or delight a child. ✌ Many a Southwestern chef has sold an entrée with a cute little saguaro cactus garnish sticking up on one side. You can also cut tortillas into small strips and fry a tangle of them as a textural garnish for a soup, dip, or salsa.

Previous page: Fruity Nachos, page 14.

BASIC BAKED CHIPS

Cut flour or corn tortillas into wedges with kitchen shears or a knife. Lay them close together but not overlapping on a baking sheet. Preheat oven to 400 degrees. Brush or spray tortillas with water or vegetable spray on the top side only. Sprinkle on seasoning, if desired (see suggested seasonings below). Bake for 7 or 8 minutes. Keep an eye on them. Remove them from the oven when they are lightly browned. The chips may darken a bit more after you take them out, and will crisp up as they cool.

SUGGESTED SEASONINGS

Olive oil spray plus Italian seasoning

Dry ranch dressing mix

Salt

Onion powder

Paprika

Cayenne

Taco seasoning

Garlic powder, by itself or combined with powdered cumin

New Mexico hot chili powder, or any of your favorite powdered Southwestern herbs or spices

Parmesan cheese

Chili powder

Seasoning mixes such as Mrs. Dash or Morton's Seasoning Blend

Use butter-flavor spray for sweet seasonings such as:

Cinnamon

Cinnamon and sugar

Sugar and powdered ginger

Sugar and freshly ground nutmeg

Spray tortilla wedges with flavored nonstick sprays such as olive oil or butter-flavor. Add salt and a light sprinkle of seasoning to heighten the flavor. Seasonings should be added to chips before they're baked (add it after, and off it falls).

FRIED CHIPS

You can fry any kind of tortilla, root vegetable, or wonton. Hot, fresh, home-fried corn tortillas are so delicious it's hard to beat them, and it's fun to offer a variety.

Because of modern diet restrictions, many people have forgotten how to fry. But instead of becoming a lost art, frying is making a comeback. If you know the basics, you can turn out light, near-greaseless tidbits that are so good your guests can't stop snacking on them.

WHAT TO FRY

Tortillas: Corn tortillas fry best of all. Flour tortillas may puff in odd ways; the flavored wraps do quite well, however.

Wontons: These make great chips, or tasty garnishes for soups and salads—an unexpected alternative to croutons—when cut into strips. Check the refrigerated section in the produce aisle for various sizes and kinds of fresh pasta wrappers, such as wonton, eggroll, and dumpling skins used in Chinese dishes.

Solid root vegetables: Potatoes, carrots, parsnips, and sweet potatoes are delicious fried into chips. The real key with vegetables is slicing them thinly enough. If they're too thick, they won't be crisp. Aim for about the thickness of a corn tortilla. Although this can be done with a knife, it is much easier if you have a mandolin. This kitchen gadget has a sharp edge built into the bottom and a mechanism on top that moves the vegetable over the edge to shave it very thin. (Cooking stores and catalogs sometimes carry the plastic, less-expensive mandolins; the kind for professional kitchens cost hundreds of dollars. Mandolins are also handy if you ever dehydrate anything from your garden.) Or use a vegetable peeler to shave vegetables into thin strips, or put them through the slicing disc in your food processor.

Opposite Top: Baked Chips, page 7, with Sweet Onion Salsa, page 50. Bottom: Fried Chips, above, with Fresh Herb Dip, page 26.

Frying oil and temperature: We prefer shortening (such as Crisco) or peanut oil, because Crisco is all-vegetable and peanut oil won't smoke at high frying temperatures. (If you like the flavor of lard, by all means, use lard. Once or twice a year.)

Fun flavoring tip: Add a little bit of hot chili oil to the oil before you fry chips (look for it in the Chinese-food aisle of your supermarket).

One of the real tricks to deep-frying is to maintain the proper temperature of the oil or shortening. For chips, the temperature is 390 degrees. For sweet potatoes and carrots, it's 365 degrees; for potatoes and parsnips, 380 degrees. Wontons are like a fresh dough and need a slightly lower 350 degrees. If you don't have a thermostat on your fryer, test the oil temperature by adding a cube of bread. It should be golden brown in sixty seconds at 365 degrees. After a little experience, you will be able to finesse the temperature. The even heat of a countertop deep-fryer or electric skillet makes frying easy. Or attach a candy thermometer to the side of a deep pot—just be sure it isn't touching the bottom of the pot.

When the oil has reached the desired temperature, add a few pieces of tortilla or vegetable. This is one of those times when you have to stand right over the stove. Let the answering machine catch the phone. Make sure the pieces don't overlap and stick together. Watch for a change in color on the bottom side of the food, then flip it over with tongs or a slotted spoon. As soon as the color is what you want, fish it out. Again, it may darken a tad after removal from the hot oil. Drain on paper towels.

Vegetables with high sugar content, such as sweet potatoes and carrots, will darken much faster than vegetables without high sugars. Potatoes have more water in them, and will tend to splatter when you first put them in the oil, so be careful not to get popped on and burned! Vegetables will get a bit crispier as they cool.

Add just a few bits of food to the oil at any one time, because if you add too many, the food will cool the oil—with greasier results.

Season chips after frying. Salt is always good, to our way of thinking. Or try any of the herb combinations mentioned above. Fried sweet potatoes are fantastic with a little salt and chili powder or brown sugar.

NACHOS

If all you know about nachos is the plastic kind sold in movie theaters and stadiums, we're here to tell you to think again. Nachos made at home can be terrific. The trick to excellent, crispy, home-made nachos is in the cheese. We like to use a premium pepper jack or even a salsa jack. The sprinkling of peppers in the cheese adds yet another chile to the topping repertoire.

OUR LIST OF POPULAR NACHO TOPPERS

Ground beef (cooked and drained)

Chicken (Cooked and shredded—use up small
   amounts of leftovers!)

Refried beans, charro beans (drained),
   black beans (drained and rinsed)

Jalapeños, green chiles, roasted poblanos

Sautéed onions, green onions, red onions, chives

Cilantro

Chopped tomatoes

Cooked tomatillos

Black olives

Cheddar cheese, jack cheese, processed cheese

Sour cream

Salsa

Assemble nachos just before broiling to reduce the risk of soggy chips. Thoroughly drain any wet ingredients such as olives. Use a light hand when sprinkling on the ingredients. Toppings shouldn't over-power or weigh down the chips.

Cooking nachos: Set the oven rack about six inches below the broiler element and preheat broiler. Assemble the nachos on a baking sheet. Once assembled, slide the pan under the broiler and keep your eye on it. Nachos are done when the cheese melts, and this can happen quickly, usually 3 to 5 minutes. For best results, never turn your back on your nachos!

Macho Nachos

Tortilla chips
About 1 cup of your favorite chili
About 1 cup grated Cheddar
    cheese
About 4 or 5 green onions,
    chopped

We give approximate amounts on nachos, because ingredients will vary depending on how much you want to make. For this particular nacho, these amounts will make one 10 x 15-inch pan of nachos. (And if you're feeding more than one man or boy, that's probably not nearly enough.)

Preheat broiler.
Layer chips on baking sheet and sprinkle with chili. Top with cheese, then green onions. Place under broiler for 3 to 5 minutes, watching closely, until cheese bubbles. Serve at once.

Almost a Meal

MAKES SEVERAL SMALL SERVINGS.

Loaded Nachos

Tortilla chips
1 (15-ounce) can black beans,
    drained
1 (4-ounce) can chopped green
    chiles or 2 tablespoons
    chopped jalapeños
1 small tomato, chopped
½ pound pepper jack or Sonoma
    jack cheese, shredded
1 cup sour cream (optional)

Don't tell anybody, but we ate these for dinner while testing them. Now they're family favorites.

Preheat broiler.
Layer chips onto two 10 x 15-inch jelly roll pans. Sprinkle with beans, chiles, and tomato. Cover evenly with cheese. Place under broiler for 3 to 5 minutes. Remove from oven and serve immediately, with a dab of sour cream on top of each loaded chip, if desired.

Almost a Meal

MAKES 3 OR 4 DINNER-SIZE SERVINGS, OR SEVERAL MORE SERVINGS AS A SNACK.

Opposite Top: Loaded Nachos. **Bottom:** Fruity Nachos, page 14.

Fruity Nachos

1 cup fresh blackberries,
  raspberries, or a combination
  of both
¼ cup Chambord (raspberry)
  liqueur
1 fresh peach, thinly sliced and
  each slice halved
¼ cup peach schnapps or
  Grand Marnier
1 cup fresh strawberries, rinsed
  and thinly sliced
¼ cup amaretto
½ cup whipped topping
½ cup sour cream
6 flour tortillas
Butter-flavored cooking spray
Sugar
Cinnamon

These strike a beautiful pose when served as a dessert. The sweet, baked tortilla chips can be used as a basis for any number of other Southwestern-style dessert variations.

In separate bowls, combine berries and Chambord, peaches and schnapps or Grand Marnier, and strawberries and amaretto. Allow fruit to marinate in the refrigerator for at least 1 hour, gently stirring every now and then.

Combine the whipped topping and sour cream in a small bowl, stirring to blend. Refrigerate.

Preheat the oven to 400 degrees.

Stack the tortillas and cut into wedges. Lightly coat wedges on one side with cooking spray and arrange in a single layer on a jelly roll pan or a pizza pan. Sprinkle with sugar and cinnamon. Bake for 7 to 8 minutes until crisp. Remove from oven and cool. (If made ahead, these keep well stored in an airtight container.)

To serve, arrange chips on a serving platter. Just before serving, load the chips with the marinated fruits, one fruit to a chip. A few slices or a couple of berries per chip is plenty. Top with a dollop of the cream mixture and serve immediately.

Entertaining

MAKES ENOUGH FOR A CROWD,
ABOUT 50 CHIPS.

Goat Cheese, Salsa, and Shrimp Nachos

When you have just a dab of fruity salsa or tomatillo salsa left, remember this recipe and make it! This is excellent with any salsa, especially the fruity ones we recommend for fish. Again, we give approximate amounts to make one pan.

Preheat broiler.

Layer chips on baking sheet. Combine cheese and milk in a cup or small container and stir well to blend. Spread mixture on chips. Dab each with a teaspoon or so of salsa. Top with one or two shrimp. Place under broiler for 3 to 5 minutes, watching closely, until cheese starts to puff. Serve at once.

Elegant

Tortilla chips to cover a
    10 x 15-inch pan.
About 5 ounces of goat cheese
2 tablespoons cream or milk
About ¼ cup of your favorite salsa
About 1 to 1½ cups medium-size
    cooked shrimp

CHIP ALTERNATIVES

Breadsticks and Pretzels

Dipping is not just for chips anymore. Any dip or salsa recipe that would work well with crackers is equally wonderful with a breadstick or a pretzel. Of course, you can buy the hard pretzels and sticks at the supermarket. But as Sam's Café has shown with the popular fresh breadsticks and pink dip in lieu of crunchy chips and saucy salsa, the warm combination of yeasty dough and savory dip is a comforting start to a great meal, or accompaniment to a cocktail and a good conversation.

We have found that the best way to the perfect dip-ready bread is baking on a stone tile. The tile creates a crisp crust with just enough reinforcement to stand up to a dip while preserving the delicious chewy center.

There are several options for working with yeast dough: the bread machine, the heavy-duty mixer equipped with a dough hook, and hand-kneading. Use the one that suits you best.

To adapt this recipe to the bread machine, add ingredients to the machine in the order recommended by the manufacturer. Reduce yeast to 1 1/2 teaspoons. Process on the dough setting. Remove dough from bread machine at the end of the dough cycle, and proceed from the first rise, below.

A tip for kneading and shaping the dough: Instead of sprinkling flour on your work surface to keep the dough from sticking, spray the surface—and your hands—with nonstick vegetable spray. It works better than flour and the dough stays tender.

2¼ teaspoons active dry yeast

2 tablespoons sugar

1 cup warm water (110 degrees)

3 to 3¼ cups unbleached
    all-purpose flour

1 teaspoon salt

1 tablespoon canola oil, plus extra
    for coating kneading surface
    and bowl

1 egg

Cornmeal to line the baking pan

Egg wash: 1 egg beaten with
    1 tablespoon water

Coarse salt, such as kosher salt
    (optional)

Caraway seeds, poppy seeds, and
    sesame seeds (optional)

In a large mixing bowl, dissolve yeast and sugar in water. Let the mixture stand until it becomes foamy, about 10 to 15 minutes. Stir in two cups of flour and add the salt, oil, and egg. Beat to a smooth texture. Add the remaining flour a bit at a time. Turn out onto an oil-coated kneading surface (or place the dough hook on the mixer) and knead until the dough is smooth and elastic.

Place in an oiled bowl, turning to coat the entire surface. Cover and let stand to rise, about 1¹/₂ hours, or until the size of the dough has doubled. Punch down the dough to deflate, cover and let rise again for about 1 hour.

On a lightly oiled surface turn out the dough and cut into twenty pieces of equal size.

For breadsticks: Roll each piece between your palms and the work surface to form an ¹/₈-inch stick. Then twist the stick by rolling the ends in opposite directions simultaneously.

For pretzels: Roll each piece between your palms and the surface into a 16- to 18-inch strand. Form into a pretzel shape by holding up the ends, allowing the middle part of the strand to touch the working surface a few inches to the left of center.

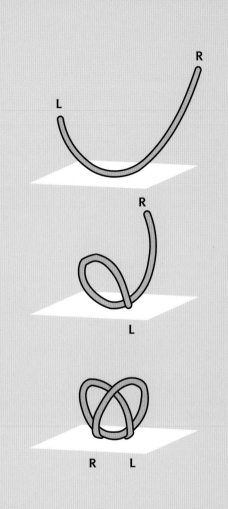

Loop the left end over to cross the right tail and tuck the end under. Cross the right side over the left loop, forming the right loop, and tuck the end under.

Sprinkle a baking sheet with cornmeal. Transfer the shaped breads to the sheet.

Using a pastry brush, coat the bread with the egg wash. Let rise about 30 minutes.

Line the oven rack with stone baking tiles and preheat to 400 degrees.

Coat the bread again with egg wash and sprinkle with salt or seeds, if using. Place the pan on the tiles in the oven and bake for about 15 minutes, until the bread begins to brown. Remove the pan from the oven and transfer the bread to the baking tiles using a spatula or tongs. Continue baking for another 5 to 10 minutes, until golden brown.

Make Ahead

MAKES ABOUT 20 BREADSTICKS OR PRETZELS.

Cheesy Corn Crackers

Okay, so these are a little bit more work than baking a chip. Make them when you want something different and special.

In a medium bowl, combine cheese, flour, cornmeal, baking powder, salt, mustard, turmeric and cumin.

Combine oil and milk and stir well with a fork. Knead briefly in the bowl until dough is cohesive. Shape dough into a ball, flatten it slightly, and wrap it in plastic wrap. Refrigerate for at least 1 hour.

Preheat oven to 350 degrees. Divide dough in half. Roll 1 batch out onto lightly floured surface to ⅛-inch thickness. Use a cookie cutter or knife to cut the dough into shapes or pieces about 2 inches in diameter. Transfer to an ungreased baking sheet and prick each piece several times with a fork. Bake until brown around the edges and lightly brown on top, about 12 to 15 minutes. Cool on racks.

Repeat the process with the remaining batch of dough, using as little additional flour as possible.

Crackers can be stored at room temperature for a few days.

Make Ahead

MAKES 4 TO 5 DOZEN.

6 ounces sharp Cheddar or pepper jack cheese, finely shredded
1 cup unbleached flour
2 tablespoons cornmeal
1 teaspoon baking powder
½ teaspoon salt
1 teaspoon dry mustard
¼ teaspoon turmeric
¼ teaspoon cumin
¼ cup oil
⅓ cup skim milk

Bagel Chips

Large bagel(s)

Have any stale bagels lying around? They're perfect for Bagel Chips! Amy Sisti figured this out when she worked at the food! section of The Arizona Republic. *You can coordinate any savory bagel flavor with a tasty dip or spread: jalapeño bagels with Pink Dip, pesto bagels with Tuscan Salsa, onion bagels with New Wave Spinach Dip. And talk about easy—all you do is slice a bagel!*

Preheat oven to 400 degrees.

Slice bagel into 1/16- to 1/8-inch-thick vertical rounds, or cut bagel in half and slice horizontally into crescents. (Note: Stale bagels are easier to cut into thin slices than fresher ones. If using fresh bagels, slice from the inner side out to the crust.) Arrange on an uncoated baking sheet in a single layer. Bake for 7 minutes. Remove and flip bagel chips so bottom side will crisp. Bake for 3 more minutes. Remove from oven.

Bagel chips will crisp more as they cool. Store, airtight, up to two days.

Make Ahead

EACH BAGEL WILL MAKE 8 TO 12 CHIPS
IF SLICED HORIZONTALLY, OR ABOUT
20 CHIPS IF SLICED VERTICALLY.

Dips

Entertaining can be easy and festive—just make a variety of dips and serve a choice of dippers. Coupled with classic cocktails or sodas, these dips not only make for a beautiful buffet but they can also stand in for a traditional meal, delighting your guests and keeping you out of the kitchen during the party.

Refried Beans for Dip

Pinto beans can be cooked and frozen in batches, so you've always got some to refry for a dip or side dish. We like them flavored with ham, but you can substitute garlic and onions. Or you can cook them without any additions and refry them in bacon drippings for flavor. The beans can be traditionally boiled, pressure-cooked, or slow-cooked.

To prepare beans for cooking:

Pick over the beans carefully, looking for stones. Wash in a colander.

Traditional method: Place the beans in a large bowl. Cover the beans with water and let soak overnight.

Quick-soak method: Place the beans in a pot. Cover with water to one inch above the beans; bring to a boil for 2 minutes. Cover the pan tightly with a lid and remove from heat. Let sit 1 hour.

To cook:

Traditional and slow-cooker method: Drain the soaking water and cover beans with fresh water. Add ham (ends from a whole ham, ham hocks, or cut pieces of ham) if using. Bring to a boil, reduce heat and simmer for 2 hours. In a slow-cooker, cook beans on high according to the manufacturer's instructions, usually 6 to 8 hours.

Previous page: New Wave Spinach Dip, page 37.

Pressure-cooker method: Consult your manufacturer's instructions. Usually, you cover beans with water in the bottom of the cooker, being careful not to fill the cooker more than half full. Some directions say to add 2 cups water for each 1 cup of beans, and 1 tablespoon oil for each cup of beans to help prevent foaming. If you have not soaked the beans, bring to a boil for 2 minutes. Cover with pressure-cooker top and remove from heat. Let cool for about 30 minutes. Remove top; drain water. Add seasonings, and water as needed to meet the requirements of your pressure-cooker. Replace the top, bring up to pressure over high heat and finish cooking according to manufacturer's instructions.

After cooking, remove any bones and skin from the ham, if used.

Refrying the beans:

When beans are cooked, remove ham. Melt $1/4$ cup lard (or vegetable or canola oil, or bacon drippings) in a heavy skillet (we prefer cast iron) on the stove. Add beans, one cup at a time, mashing with a potato masher. Stir often, scraping the bottom of the pan until the beans are smooth and creamy.

For dip:

Add about $1/2$ cup shredded longhorn cheddar cheese to 2 cups of beans and stir to melt. And, if you like, stir in $1/2$ cup of your favorite tomato-based salsa or hot sauce. Top with additional shredded cheese and a dollop of sour cream just before serving.

Souper Shrimp Dip

1 (10½-ounce) can cream of
    shrimp soup
8 ounces cream cheese, softened
1 (4-ounce) can baby shrimp,
    drained
2 celery ribs, finely chopped
Louisiana Hot Sauce to taste

When Jacquie Weedon came up with this luscious dip, her husband, Walt, proceeded to eat the whole bowl!

Mix all ingredients in a medium bowl and blend. Chill for 1 hour.

Have on Hand

MAKES ABOUT 3½ CUPS (OR 1 SERVING!).

Spicy Bean Dip

Dried poblano chiles: 1 for mild,
    2 for medium, 3 for hot
¾ cup hot water
1 cup refried beans
3 tablespoons plain yogurt
3 tablespoons grated longhorn or
    Cheddar cheese

Substitute dried chipotles or another hot, red, dried pepper if you can't find dried poblanos.

Cover chiles with hot water and soak for about an hour, or until the chiles are soft. Drain and place in a food processor or blender with the remaining ingredients and purée until smooth. Transfer to a microwavable bowl and microwave on high for 2 minutes, or until piping hot. Serve immediately with chips.

Chafing Dish

MAKES ABOUT 1 CUP.

Simple Green Dip

Make this super-simple dip non-fat by substituting fat-free sour cream.

Combine ingredients in a small bowl. Chill for at least 30 minutes. Served, chilled, with chips or vegetables.

Super Easy

MAKES 1 CUP.

1 cup sour cream
1 (4-ounce) can chopped green chiles
Garlic powder to taste (optional)

Southwestern Hummus

The quintessential Middle Eastern purée, hummus, is everywhere these days. Our Southwestern version is delicious on lavash crackers, pita bread, bagel chips, or raw vegetables. Pepperoncini and Greek olives make a nice garnish for major noshing events.

Place all ingredients in a blender or food processor and blend to desired consistency. Use water from rehydrating chipotle if needed to thin. Serve topped with a little olive oil and paprika or cayenne.

Don't Miss!

MAKES ABOUT 2 CUPS.

Note: The spicy heat of this hummus increases as the flavors meld, so if you like hot flavors, you will like this spread even more after a day or two in the fridge.

1 teaspoon crushed garlic (or more to taste)
1 (15-ounce) can garbanzo beans, drained
3 tablespoons lemon juice
2 tablespoons olive oil
¼ teaspoon ground cumin
Salt to taste
Cayenne to taste
½ cup tahini (sesame seed paste, available in Middle Eastern and health food stores)
½ to 1 dried chipotle chile (rehydrated in hot water, water reserved), or chipotle in adobo sauce
Paprika for garnish

Chihuahua Couscous Spread

½ cup couscous
⅝ cup boiling water
1 (15-ounce) can black beans,
  drained
1 chipotle chile pepper in
  adobo sauce
½ cup plain yogurt

Serve this unusually textured dip with a knife for spreading on crackers or baked flour tortilla chips.

Pour water over couscous and stir to combine. Let set at least 5 minutes, or until cool. Fluff with a fork.

Purée beans and pepper in a blender or food processor. Stir in yogurt. Add to the couscous, stirring to blend. Serve promptly.

Almost a Meal

MAKES 1½ CUPS.

Fresh Herb Dip

½ cup sour cream
½ cup plain nonfat yogurt
¼ to ⅓ cup finely chopped fresh
  herbs (your choice)
Garlic powder to taste (optional)
Salt and pepper to taste

Use any single fresh herb or combination of herbs in this dip, such as basil, oregano, and thyme. If you include rosemary, use less because it's strong and will overpower other herbs. To turn this into a salad dressing, thin it with a bit of milk.

Combine all ingredients in a small bowl. Cover and chill for up to 8 hours before serving with raw vegetables, chips, or crackers.

Versatile

MAKES A LITTLE MORE THAN 1 CUP.

Kathy's Guacamole

Kathy Blake-Novotny is a native Arizonan whose years of tasting other versions of guacamole led to her own special version.

In a medium bowl, mash avocados with a fork, leaving them somewhat chunky. Combine with remaining ingredients. Serve promptly with lots of fresh tortilla chips.

Entertaining

MAKES ABOUT 1½ CUPS.

2 ripe medium avocados
1½ tablespoons Kathy's Salsa (recipe page 62) or other salsa
⅓ cup hot Mexican-style tomato sauce, such as El Pato brand, or ⅓ cup tomato sauce combined with 1 teaspoon hot sauce
1 teaspoon minced red onion
1 teaspoon minced fresh jalapeño
1 teaspoon fresh lime juice
Salt and pepper to taste

Sonoran Strata

Our variation on the favorite Seven-Layer Dip is easier and more flavorful! Always a big hit at parties.

In a food processor or blender purée beans, chipotle, and garlic powder. Spread in a clear serving bowl or onto a serving platter and level the top with a spatula.

Mash avocados with lime juice, garlic powder, and salt. Spread carefully on top of the bean layer.

Spread tomatoes or salsa on top of avocado. Sprinkle evenly with cheese.

Serve with sturdy tortilla chips. Provide a knife to encourage dipping down through all the layers.

Entertaining

MAKES ABOUT 3 CUPS.

1 (15-ounce) can black beans, drained but not rinsed
½ to 1 chipotle pepper, dried and rehydrated, or chipotle in adobo sauce
Garlic powder to taste
2 ripe avocados
Juice of one lime
Salt to taste
1 large, ripe tomato, chopped, or 1 cup fresh tomato salsa
1 cup crumbled Mexican cotija cheese or farmer's cheese

Pollo Con Queso

½ cup chicken, cooked and
   shredded
¼ cup chopped onion
2 small tomatoes, chopped
1 tablespoon chopped jalapeños
8 ounces pasteurized process
   cheese spread, cubed

Note about hot, cheese-based dips: Queso
dips vary in consistency with their temperature. After heating, the cheese mixture will
be thin, and will thicken as it cools. Serve
hot cheese dips in a slow cooker, fondue
pot, or a microwavable dish to facilitate
reheating.

*Cheese-based dips are common in Southwestern-style
noshing. The addition of chicken makes this one a bit more
substantial. There are those who will no doubt find it a
meal in itself.*

Mix all ingredients in a small microwavable bowl. Heat on
high power for 4 minutes. Stir well. Let stand for a few minutes before serving.

Almost a Meal

MAKES 2 CUPS.

Variation: Substitute 1 cup of your favorite salsa for the onion, tomato, and jalapeño.

Pistachio Beef Spread

¾ cup cubed roast beef
½ cup mayonnaise
2 tablespoons chopped onion
2 tablespoons sweet pickle relish
2 tablespoons chopped celery
½ cup chopped pistachios

*This hearty recipe can be used for a sandwich filling,
a spread, or a dip. Use your imagination.*

Combine all ingredients except nuts in a food processor or
blender. Pulse until blended. Stir in pistachios.

Almost a Meal

MAKES 1 CUP.

Opposite (clockwise from upper left): Southwestern Hummus, page 25; Fresh Herb Dip,
page 26; Sonoran Strata, page 27; Kathy's Guacamole, page 27.

White Bean Pâté y Mole

½ dried poblano or chipotle chile
    (a whole one if you like it hot)
1 (15-ounce) can Great Northern
    beans, rinsed and drained
2 tablespoons plain yogurt
1 teaspoon dried oregano
2 cloves garlic
Salt and pepper to taste
2 tablespoons mole sauce
⅛ cup vegetable broth

The commercial version of mole is a Mexican relation to tahini, since it contains sesame seeds. But it also has peanut butter and chocolate! Savory mole sauce is especially great over chicken enchiladas or other chicken dishes, and it makes a nice contrast to the zippy pâté in this recipe as well. You can find it in the Mexican food section of the supermarket or specialty store.

Reconstitute the chile by soaking in boiling water until the water is cool. Drain and remove the seeds. Place the chile, beans, yogurt, oregano, garlic, and salt and pepper in a blender or food processor. Pulse for about 2 minutes, or until the mixture is slightly lumpy. Place the mixture in a parchment-lined, 2-cup mold. Chill for a couple of hours, and invert on a serving dish. Remove parchment. (Or, if you're serving it right away, simply mound pâté on a serving dish.)

Just before you're ready to serve, place the mole sauce in a small microwave-safe dish. Stir in about 2 teaspoons of the broth. Heat for thirty seconds on high in the microwave. Remove from the microwave and stir in the remaining broth. Pour over the pâté.

Serve immediately with corn or flour tortilla chips or water crackers.

Elegant

MAKES ABOUT 2 CUPS.

Hot Cheese, Mushroom, and Chorizo Dip

Judy and Anita Mabante Leach had to recreate this spectacular combination of flavors when it was removed from the menu of their favorite Mexican lunch restaurant. The ease of preparation makes it an ideal dip for parties.

12 ounces Mexican asadero or
    Monterey jack cheese,
    cut into chunks
6 ounces mushrooms, sliced
1 cup chorizo, cooked and well
    drained
2 green onions, chopped, or
    ¼ cup finely chopped
    white onion

Combine all ingredients in a 2-quart microwavable bowl. Heat at 70 percent power in microwave for 3 minutes. Remove and stir well. Heat again at 70 percent power for 2 minutes. Stir and check to determine if cheese is melted. If not, continue heating at one minute intervals, stirring after each minute. When all the cheese is melted, the mixture will have a uniform color. Serve immediately with tortilla chips.

Chafing Dish

MAKES ABOUT 3 CUPS.

Note: For a buffet, keep warm over heat or in a slow cooker. Or serve half and keep the rest, covered, in a 250-degree oven until ready to serve. If needed, thin with a couple of tablespoons of sour cream.

See note, page 28, about hot, cheese-based dips.

Southwest Chicken Spread

8 ounces cream cheese
1 (15-ounce) can black beans, drained well
3 green onions, thinly sliced
2 tablespoons roasted, salted sunflower seeds, plus extra for garnish (optional)
8 ounces (1 cup) sour cream
1 cup cooked, chopped chicken (or 8 ounces canned)
2 tablespoons chopped cilantro

Carol Buto's regional version of her Caviar Cream Cheese Spread (page 33) is just as delicious. The sunflower seeds add a nice note of crunchiness. Your guests will love this.

Spread cream cheese on a dinner-size serving plate. Top with black beans, onions, and sunflower seeds. Spread on sour cream. Sprinkle with chicken, cilantro, and, if desired, a few extra sunflower seeds for garnish.

Serve with crackers.

Elegant

MAKES ABOUT 4 CUPS.

Bleu Cheese Spread with Nuts

4 ounces bleu cheese
4 ounces cream cheese
¼ cup chopped toasted almonds or pecans
1 tablespoon dry sherry or brandy (optional)

An excellent choice for a holiday buffet. Or pack into small bowls or crocks as holiday gifts for bleu cheese lovers.

In a medium bowl or a food processor, thoroughly mix cheeses and sherry (if using). Mound onto a serving dish and sprinkle with nuts.

Serve with fresh pears and crackers.

Make Ahead

MAKES ABOUT 1¼ CUPS.

Option: Mix nuts into cheeses if packing into a crock.

Caviar Cream Cheese Spread

Carol Buto, who creates prize-winning interiors in Scottsdale and the rest of Arizona, serves this stunning creation at her annual Christmas party. We can't even begin to tell you how delicious and beautiful it is—you just have to try it for yourself to see.

8 ounces cream cheese

2 hard-cooked eggs, finely chopped

3 green onions, thinly sliced

1 teaspoon capers

8 ounces sour cream

2 ounces red caviar, drained in a fine sieve

Spread cream cheese on a dinner-size serving plate. Sprinkle with eggs, then onions, then capers, then sour cream. At this point, the spread can be covered and chilled for a few hours before serving.

Just before serving, top with caviar. Serve with water crackers.

Elegant

MAKES ABOUT 2½ CUPS.

Carne Con Queso

16 ounces pasteurized process
cheese spread with jalapeño
(Mexican style), cubed
12 ounces (about a cup) roast
beef, cubed and shredded
¼ cup onion, chopped
1 large tomato, chopped

This beef version of cheese dip is heartier than the most of the genre, making it ideal for appetizer parties. Use your own leftover roast beef, roast beef from the deli case, or even canned roast beef in gravy. Drain the gravy and shred the beef for the right consistency.

Mix all ingredients in a microwavable bowl. Heat on high power for 4 minutes. Stir well. Let stand for a few minutes before serving.

Almost a Meal

MAKES 2 CUPS.

See note, page 28, about hot, cheese-based dips.

Variation: Substitute 1 cup of your favorite salsa for the onion and tomato and use cheese without jalapeños.

Cranberry Chicken Spread

¾ cup cubed and shredded
chicken (or 6 ounces canned
chicken)
¼ cup cashew pieces
2 tablespoons chopped celery
½ cup mayonnaise
¼ cup sweetened dried
cranberries

Water crackers or cracker thins made from various nuts make fine dippers for this light, cool version of chicken salad. Or use it to make lovely finger sandwiches for a tea or shower.

Combine all ingredients in a medium bowl, mix, and chill well. Use as a dip, a spread, or a sandwich filling.

Almost a Meal

MAKES 1¼ CUPS.

Pink Dip

Two ingredients? It can't be! But it is! Sam's Café, the popular Southwestern chain based in Dallas, serves this with fresh, hot breadsticks, such as those on page 17, when you arrive at your table. Our version is lower in fat, especially when served with fresh vegetables.

Bring the cheese to room temperature. Combine with salsa in a food processor or blender and process until smooth and pink, at least two minutes. Chill until served.

Serve with chips or fresh, warm breadsticks.

Super Easy

MAKES ABOUT 2 CUPS.

12 ounces Neufchâtel cheese
1 cup mild salsa, such as Pace brand

Baked Crab-and-Cheese Dip

This is the first thing that disappears every time Sarah Staley takes it to a party—which is often!

Combine all ingredients in a large bowl, stirring thoroughly. Place in a 13 x 9-inch baking dish coated with nonstick cooking spray.

Bake at 350 degrees for 40 minutes. Serve with crackers—Wheat Thins are excellent—or toasted baguette slices.

Festive

MAKES ABOUT 5 CUPS.

2 (8-ounce) packages cream cheese
2 (6-ounce) cans crab meat, drained
4 tablespoons lemon juice or lime juice
4 dashes Worcestershire sauce
4 dashes Louisiana Hot Sauce
16 ounces Cheddar cheese, grated

Sour Cream and Mushroom Spread

A must for mushroom lovers.

Heat olive oil in a large skillet and sauté onion until translucent. Add mushrooms and Worcestershire, salt, pepper, and garlic powder. As the mushrooms cook they will release liquid; cook until the liquid evaporates.

Let the mixture cool a bit, then place in a medium bowl. Add sour cream and combine. Adjust seasoning. Serve immediately, with crackers.

Chafing Dish

MAKES ABOUT 2 CUPS.

2 tablespoons olive oil
1 large onion, chopped (about
    1¼ cups)
12 ounces mushrooms, sliced
1 tablespoon Worcestershire Sauce
Salt and pepper to taste
Garlic powder to taste
1 cup light sour cream

New Wave Spinach Dip

A twist on the now-classic vegetable-soup mix spinach dip found at many parties. Yes, you can serve it in the center of a hollowed-out round of bread. It is also fantastic with raw vegetables.

Combine all ingredients in a large bowl. Chill for at least 4 hours to let flavors develop. Serve in a bread bowl or with a variety of crackers.

Make Ahead

MAKES ABOUT 5 CUPS.

1 (1-ounce) packet onion soup mix
10 ounces frozen, chopped
    spinach, thawed, drained well,
    squeezed dry
¼ cup finely chopped red bell
    pepper
¼ cup finely chopped green bell
    pepper
¼ cup finely chopped carrot
2 cups sour cream
1 cup mayonnaise
1 (4-ounce) can water chestnuts,
    chopped
1 ripe medium tomato, chopped

Opposite (clockwise from upper left): Hot Cheese, Mushroom, and Chorizo Dip, page 31; White Bean Pâté y Mole, page 30; Cranberry Chicken Spread, page 34; Southwest Chicken Spread, page 32.

Feta and Rosemary Spread

4 ounces feta cheese, crumbled
1 tablespoon fresh rosemary, finely
  chopped
4 ounces Neufchâtel cheese
2 cloves garlic, minced

*Once we made this, we couldn't get it out of our minds!
It is really good.*

Place all ingredients in a food processor. Pulse until mixed.
Transfer to a bowl. Serve with water crackers.

Don't Miss!

MAKES 1 CUP.

Monterey Jack and Poblano Dip

1 pound Monterey jack cheese,
  shredded
¾ cup sour cream
3 large poblano chiles, roasted,
  peeled, and diced
4 green onions, diced
½ teaspoon hot pepper sauce
  (or to taste)
Black pepper, to taste

*"This stuff is better than chocolate!" said Judy's son,
Mack, after eating it the first time. We think only the most
hardened chocoholics would disagree.*

In a medium-size microwavable bowl, heat cheese at 50
percent power for 3 minutes to melt. Stir in remaining ingredients. Taste for seasoning and temperature. You will likely
need to microwave again at 50 percent power for 2 additional
minutes.

Serve hot with tortilla chips.

Chafing Dish

MAKES ABOUT 3 CUPS.

Salmon Spread

This classic number was a hit among the ladies at a recent "Buffet at a Boutique" party. The party—and the spread—were conceived and masterfully executed by Cherilee "CC" Churchill of Scottsdale.

In a medium bowl, whip all the ingredients except pepper together with an electric hand mixer. Transfer to a serving bowl and garnish with cracked pepper. Refrigerate overnight. Serve chilled with toast rounds or cocktail breads.

Make Ahead

MAKES ABOUT 2 CUPS.

2 (6-ounce) cans skinless, boneless pink salmon, drained
8 ounces cream cheese, softened
1 tablespoon Dijon mustard
¼ teaspoon liquid smoke (or to taste)
¼ teaspoon salt
Freshly cracked black pepper

Clam Dip

Reminiscent of the seafood cocktails sold in sundae cups along the Mexican coastline, this rich dip is a nice alternative to standard salsa.

Place all ingredients in a medium bowl and stir to combine thoroughly. Chill for two hours. Serve with crackers.

Festive

MAKES ABOUT 1½ CUPS.

8 small cloves of garlic, minced
1 teaspoon dried oregano, ground
3 tablespoons lemon juice
⅛ teaspoon crushed red pepper flakes or chile pequins
1 (6-ounce) can tomato paste
Dash Sweet and Low or 1 teaspoon sugar
½ cup chopped clams
1 tablespoon clam juice
¼ cup finely chopped celery

Artichoke Heart's Secret

1 (13½-ounce) can artichoke
    hearts, drained and chopped
8 ounces cream cheese, softened
2 tablespoons mayonnaise
3 teaspoons wasabi paste

The spicy zip in this new version of a standard dip comes from wasabi, Japanese horseradish. Wasabi can be purchased in dried form or as a paste in most supermarkets, and in Asian markets. This recipe calls for the paste, which can be made by mixing the dried version with water according to the package instructions. Serve with rice crackers or raw vegetables.

In a medium bowl blend all ingredients thoroughly.

Don't Miss!

MAKES 2 CUPS.

Jan's Shrimp Spread

1 (10¾-ounce) can tomato soup
2 (¼-ounce) envelopes unflavored
    gelatin
¾ cup water
8 ounces cream cheese
1 cup finely chopped celery
½ cup finely chopped green pepper
½ cup minced onion
½ teaspoon salt
1 cup chopped pecans
2 cups cooked, chopped shrimp
1 cup mayonnaise

Judy's cousin, Jan Trower, has delighted her family with this Shrimp Spread for years now. We all love it.

In a medium saucepan, heat soup. In a separate bowl, dissolve gelatin in water and add to hot soup. Add cream cheese and simmer, stirring, until smooth. Remove from heat. Allow to cool and add remaining ingredients. Turn into serving bowl. Refrigerate for at least 6 hours.
    Serve with crackers.

Entertaining

MAKES ABOUT 5 CUPS.

Opposite (clockwise from upper left): New Wave Spinach Dip, page 37; Monterey Jack and Poblano Dip, page 38; Strawberry Almond Crème, page 43; Basil Avocado Chutney, page 42.

Basil Avocado Chutney

2 cups packed basil leaves
⅓ cup blanched almonds
1 clove garlic, peeled
1 tablespoon fresh lemon juice
1 avocado, peeled and diced
Salt to taste

Home economist Elaine Bell graciously shared one of her late-summer creations. Make this when your basil is abundant! Tremendous with black beans and rice, meats, or fish, or use it to jazz up a so-so soup.

In a food processor, combine basil, almonds, garlic, and lemon juice. Pulse motor once or twice until the almonds are finely ground. Add the avocado and salt. Combine well. Refrigerate any leftovers. Colors will darken with storage, but taste is still superlative.

Versatile

MAKES ABOUT 1½ CUPS.

Dip for Cantaloupe

1 cup non-dairy topping or
    whipped cream
3 teaspoons ground cinnamon
½ cantaloupe, cubed

Simple and surprisingly delightful!

Place topping or cream in a small bowl. Sprinkle with cinnamon. Place the bowl on a serving platter and surround with cantaloupe.

Have on Hand

MAKES 1 CUP OF DIP.

South-of-the-Border Broccoli

"This is George Bush's least favorite dip," Mary Stutsman said. *She serves this hot cheese dip at parties in a slow-cooker. This is another recipe that easily lives in your pantry and freezer, ready for instant entertaining.*

Heat oil in a large skillet and add onion. Cook and stir, then add broccoli. Cook until both are fragrant. Pour into slow-cooker. Add cheese and tomatoes to cooker. Turn to high until melted and smooth, stirring often. When melted, turn to low heat.

   Serve with wheat crackers, vegetables, or corn chips.

Chafing Dish

MAKES ABOUT 6 CUPS.

2 teaspoons vegetable oil
1 large onion, chopped
1 (10-ounce) package chopped frozen broccoli, thawed
2 pounds pasteurized processed cheese, cut into chunks
1 (10-ounce) can Mexican-style tomatoes with onions and chiles

See note, page 28, about hot, cheese-based dips.

Strawberry Almond Crème

To make this great dip for fluffy pieces of angel food cake nonfat, use nonfat sour cream and yogurt.

In a small bowl, fold strawberries into sour cream. Fold in yogurt. Gently stir in almond extract and sugar. Chill in the freezer for 20 minutes (set a timer!) then move to the refrigerator for 1 hour. Serve with cake or mixed berries.

Elegant

MAKES ¾ CUP.

½ cup puréed strawberries (process about 12 to 15 small berries in a blender or food processor)
½ cup sour cream
½ cup plain yogurt
¼ teaspoon almond extract
2 tablespoons confectioners' sugar

Desert Dip

2 cups sour cream
2 teaspoons vanilla
¾ cup apricot or peach preserves
Sugar to taste

A bowl filled with this dip surrounded by mixed fruit pieces makes a beautiful presentation. A wonderful mid-summer cooler, especially if you live in the desert.

Combine first three ingredients in a medium bowl and blend. Sweeten with sugar and stir to combine. Chill.

Have on Hand

MAKES ABOUT 3 CUPS.

Salsas

Salsas are showing up at all stages of the meal—appetizer, main dish, and even dessert. Try dressing up eggs in the morning with a fresh salsa for huevos rancheros! The potential for salsa is limited only by our imagination.

Framboise Salsa for Grilled Halibut

3 ounces fresh raspberries
1 shallot, finely diced
2 tablespoons finely diced red
    bell pepper
1 jalapeño, seeded and finely
    chopped
2 tablespoons rice vinegar
1 tablespoon chopped fresh
    parsley
Juice of ½ lime
Salt to taste
4 grilled halibut steaks (or other
    firm white fish)

This fresh, summery salsa is a tart-sweet contrast to the flaky grilled halibut. For meals in hot summer, it's quick, easy, and cool.

Combine all ingredients except halibut in a small bowl and chill for 1 hour.

    Serve mounded over grilled fish steaks.

Elegant

MAKES 4 SERVINGS.

Serrano Mango Salsa

1 mango, diced
½ cup diced red onion
1 serrano chile, seeded and
    finely diced
Juice of 1 lime
Salt to taste

Previous page: Sweet Onion Salsa,
page 50.

This simple salsa, good cold or at room temperature, is very refreshing on a hot afternoon. We like its fruity flavor with pinot grigio and flour tortilla chips.

Combine all ingredients in a medium bowl and chill briefly.

Versatile

MAKES ABOUT 1½ CUPS.

Fresh Pantry Salsa

This spicy number lives in your pantry! The taste is hot, peppy, and fresh. Try it with scrambled eggs or as an accompaniment to grilled meats. If you can't find hot-style tomato sauce, use regular tomato sauce and add 1 teaspoon hot sauce.

1 (7-ounce) can Mexican hot-style tomato sauce such as El Pato
1 (15-ounce) can chopped tomatoes
1 (4-ounce) can diced green chiles
½ cup diced red onion
Salt and pepper to taste

Mix all ingredients in a medium bowl and chill for at least 1 hour.

Serve with tortilla chips or as a table condiment.

Have on Hand

MAKES ABOUT 3 CUPS.

Jicama Salsa

Once considered exotic, jicama is now a staple on the appetizer circuit. But you can take jicama way beyond the crudité tray. Try this crunchy combination on top of mixed greens for a luscious salad that requires no dressing.

¾ cup peeled, diced jicama
½ cup diced red onion
3 tablespoons chopped cilantro
1 jalapeño, seeded and diced
Juice of 1 lime
1 teaspoon sugar or ½ packet artificial sweetener (such as Sweet and Low)

Combine all ingredients in a medium bowl. Chill 1 hour.

Versatile

MAKES 1 CUP.

Sweet Tomato Salsa

12 red, vine-ripened cherry
    tomatoes, diced
½ chopped red onion
⅓ cup finely diced yellow bell
    pepper
1 jalapeño, diced
3 tablespoons red wine vinegar

*This delicate salsa is good for dipping and terrific on top of
shredded lettuce for a no-fat salad.*

Combine all ingredients in a medium bowl and chill at least
30 minutes.

Stir and Serve

MAKES ABOUT 2 CUPS.

Classic Salsa

2 very ripe tomatoes, diced
1 small onion, diced
1 small red bell pepper, diced
1 jalapeño, diced
3 cloves garlic, minced
1 (7-ounce) can tomato sauce
1 (4-ounce) can chopped green
    chiles
Salt to taste

Optional additions (Use any or all):
1 cup cooked or canned black
    beans
½ cup corn
¼ cup sliced ripe olives
¼ cup chopped cilantro

*You want a great basic salsa? Here it is, with several
variations to make it your own. This salsa is great at room
temperature.*

Combine ingredients in a medium bowl and serve.

Traditional

MAKES ABOUT 2 CUPS (WITHOUT OPTIONS).

Opposite (clockwise from upper left): Framboise Salsa for Grilled Halibut, page 46;
Serrano Mango Salsa, page 46; Cantaloupe Salsa, page 50; Jicama Salsa, page 47.

Cantaloupe Salsa

½ cantaloupe, peeled and finely
    diced
1 red bell pepper, finely diced
1 green bell pepper, finely diced
1 jalapeño, seeded and finely
    diced
1 (8-ounce) can crushed
    pineapple, with juice
Salt to taste

Kim's mother, Jacquie Weedon, invented this salsa, which was a big hit at a small dinner party. You can use it on any kind of grilled fish or chicken.

Combine all ingredients gently in a medium bowl and chill at least 1 hour.

Versatile

MAKES ABOUT 4 CUPS.

Sweet Onion Salsa

1 sweet onion, such as Vidalia or
    Walla-Walla, chopped
¼ red bell pepper, chopped
5 six-inch feathery fennel stalks,
    chopped
2 tablespoons seasoned rice vinegar
½ teaspoon salt
¼ teaspoon freshly ground
    black pepper
1 teaspoon sugar

Fennel, beloved by Italians, deserves a wider American audience. We served this onion relish at a salsa party, where it was voted a favorite. It's fabulous on a grilled burger.

Combine all ingredients in a small bowl and chill for 1 hour.

Don't Miss!

MAKES ABOUT 1½ CUPS.

Black Bean and Corn Salsa

Who would have believed black beans and corn would become salsa staples? This is very good when made a day ahead.

Combine all ingredients and chill at least 1 hour.

Stir and Serve

MAKES ABOUT 3 CUPS.

1 (15-ounce) can black beans, drained and rinsed
¾ cup whole-kernel corn, drained
½ habanero pepper, finely minced
2 cloves garlic, minced
3 scallions, sliced
2 tablespoons diced red bell pepper
1 small tomato, diced
2 tablespoons diced sweet onion, such as Vidalia
1 teaspoon salt
½ teaspoon freshly ground black pepper
1 tablespoon chopped cilantro
1 teaspoon dried oregano
1 tablespoon olive oil
2 tablespoons red wine vinegar

Peach and Fresh Ginger Salsa

This salsa is as delicious with chicken as it is with chips.

Combine all ingredients in a medium bowl and stir well. Chill at least 1 hour.

Versatile

MAKES ABOUT 2 CUPS.

2 peaches, peeled and cubed
3 tomatoes, seeded and diced
¼ cup sliced green onions
2 teaspoons sugar
2 teaspoons cider vinegar
1 teaspoon grated fresh ginger
Salt and freshly ground black pepper

Roasted Rainbow Salsa

3 large green chiles, such as
    Anaheims or poblanos
2 large firm tomatoes
1 yellow onion
1 red onion
1 head garlic
1 red bell pepper
1 yellow bell pepper
1 green bell pepper
½ cup chopped cilantro
Juice of ½ lemon
1 clove fresh garlic, minced
Salt and pepper to taste

The deep, smoky flavor of roasted vegetables makes this hearty salsa a fine accompaniment for huevos rancheros or egg dishes. It's best when made a day ahead to allow the flavors to mellow.

Spray grill with cooking spray to prevent sticking and preheat to high.

Place whole vegetables directly on the grill and roast the chiles, tomatoes, onions, garlic, and peppers, turning frequently, until the skins are charred all over.

Remove the vegetables from the grill and place in a brown paper bag or a large bowl. Fold the bag over or cover the bowl and let sit at least 15 minutes, until vegetables are cool enough to handle. The charred skins should easily slip off the chiles, tomatoes, and peppers. Use a paring knife to help remove the outer layers of the onions and garlic.

Cut vegetables into large chunks and place in a food processor or blender. Gently pulse to the desired consistency (do not overprocess). Place in a large bowl and add cilantro, lemon juice, fresh garlic, salt, and pepper. Chill at least 4 hours, preferably overnight.

Make Ahead

MAKES ABOUT 4 CUPS.

Pickled Garlic Salsa

Have you tried pickled garlic yet? It's worth seeking out in specialty stores if you can't find it in supermarkets. Kim's daughter, Melanie, is hooked on it. Serve with bagel chips, on top of hot pasta, or a salad.

Combine ingredients in a medium bowl and stir.

Super Easy

MAKES ABOUT 3 CUPS.

1 (12-ounce) jar roasted red peppers, drained and coarsely chopped
1 (5-ounce) jar pickled garlic, drained and coarsley chopped
2 tablespoons balsamic vinegar

Tuscan Salsa

The beautiful colors in this salsa are a feast for the eyes and a nice contrast to tomato salsas on a buffet. Good at room temperature or chilled.

Combine all ingredients gently in a medium bowl.

Elegant

MAKES ABOUT 2 CUPS.

1 (15-ounce) can cannellini or Great Northern beans, rinsed and drained
1 serrano chile, finely chopped
4 marinated baby carrots, sliced*
2 tablespoons chopped sweet onion, such as Vidalia
2 tablespoons chopped red onion
2 teaspoons chopped fresh thyme, lemon thyme, or ¾ teaspoon dried
Juice of ½ lemon
1 teaspoon salt
2 teaspoons hazelnut or olive oil

*Look for marinated baby carrots in gourmet food stores.

Salsa de Lupita

4 large red tomatoes
4 tomatillos
6 to 8 jalapeños
1 teaspoon chopped cilantro
1½ teaspoons salt
½ teaspoon black pepper
½ teaspoon lemon juice

Traditional and delicious, this prize-winning salsa is the creation of Lupita Banuelos of Phoenix.

Toast the tomatoes, tomatillos and jalapeños on a hot griddle on the stove until the outer skins are black. Let steam 15 minutes in a covered bowl. Remove skins. Chop and combine in a medium bowl with the rest of the ingredients.

Traditional

MAKES ABOUT 2 CUPS.

Cowboy Caviar

5 Roma tomatoes, chopped
1 (15-ounce) can corn, drained
1 (15-ounce) can black-eyed peas, drained
1 (15-ounce) can kidney beans, drained
1 (15-ounce) can cannellini or Great Northern beans, drained
1 (7-ounce) can diced green chiles
6 green onions, sliced
½ teaspoon garlic salt
1 teaspoon chili powder
½ teaspoon cumin
Juice of 2 or 3 limes
Lime slices for garnish

Our family's celebration of the 110th Frontier Days in Prescott, Arizona, was even more fun with Sharon Cooper's contribution to the annual potluck barbecue. This is a great recipe to take to a big party, because it makes a lot!

Combine tomatoes, corn, beans, chiles, and onions in a large bowl. Mix seasonings with lime juice in a small bowl or jar and pour over the bean mixture. Serve garnished with lime slices.

Entertaining

MAKES ABOUT 8 CUPS.

Arizona Caviar

Bev Walker's version of black bean and corn salsa has a perfect balance of flavors. We like it best with the optional avocados. This is great on burgers.

In a large bowl mix vinegar, garlic, and Tabasco. Add remaining ingredients and mix gently but thoroughly. Refrigerate for a few hours or overnight, stirring occasionally.

Versatile

MAKES ABOUT 5 CUPS.

4 tablespoons red wine vinegar
2 or 3 cloves garlic, chopped or minced
4 teaspoons Tabasco sauce (or more if you like it hot!)
2 (15-ounce) cans black beans, drained and rinsed
2 (11-ounce) cans corn, drained and rinsed
6 tomatoes, chopped
4 green onions, chopped
2 avocados, chopped (optional)
Salt and pepper to taste
Chopped cilantro to taste (we like at least ½ cup)

Strawberry Salsa

A wonderful way to dress up pound cake or ice cream!

Place strawberries and bananas in a medium bowl and cover with lime juice. Add remaining ingredients and gently stir to combine. Chill for no more than 1 hour.

Versatile

MAKES ABOUT 3 CUPS.

1 pint strawberries, hulled and sliced
2 large or 3 small bananas, peeled and sliced
Juice of one lime
1 teaspoon finely chopped or grated fresh ginger
½ cup unsweetened coconut
1 kiwi, sliced
2 tablespoons powdered sugar

Roasted Salsa

Roasting caramelizes the sugars in vegetables, deepening the flavors. It's another step, but well worth the effort. Make this a day ahead for the best results.

Preheat oven to 350 degrees. Lightly coat the tomatoes, onions, and garlic with vegetable spray and place on a roasting pan also lightly coated with vegetable spray. Roast until vegetables are browned, about 30 minutes. Remove from oven and let cool. Pour pan juices into a large bowl. Chop the tomatoes, removing brown parts if desired. Chop onions and squeeze garlic paste from the head.

Place vegetables and garlic paste in a large bowl with the juices from the pan. Add remaining ingredients and stir to combine. Refrigerate overnight.

Make Ahead

MAKES ABOUT 3 CUPS.

8 tomatoes, halved
2 large onions, peeled and halved
1 head of garlic, top cut off
Vegetable spray
2 (4-ounce) cans chopped green chiles
2 tablespoons balsamic vinegar
¼ cup olive oil
Juice of 1 lime
¼ teaspoon freshly ground black pepper
1 tablespoon hot sauce (we like Durkee's in this)
Dash of cumin
Salt to taste
¼ teaspoon ground chile pequins or chile tepíns (optional)

Opposite (clockwise from upper left): Sweet Onion Salsa, page 50; Black Bean and Corn Salsa, page 51; Salsa de Lupita, page 54; Tuscan Salsa, page 53.

Green Salsa with Cucumbers and Avocados

4 large cucumbers, peeled and
    seeded
3 avocados, diced
Juice of 2 limes
¼ cup chopped cilantro
¾ cup sour cream
½ cup low-fat mayonnaise
Garlic powder to taste
Freshly ground black pepper to
    taste

Creamy avocados are the perfect counterpoint to the diced cucumbers in this superlative recipe.

If not serving right away, sprinkle the cucumbers with salt and drain in a colander as long as 2 hours. If serving right away, skip this step. When cucumbers are drained, rinse them in cool water and pat them dry.

Dice cucumbers. In a large bowl, cover the avocado with the lime juice. Gently stir in cilantro. In a small bowl combine the sour cream, mayonnaise, garlic powder, and pepper. Add cucumbers and sour cream mixture to the avocados. Gently stir to combine the ingredients thoroughly. If you skipped the salting, more salt may be needed at this point.

Stir again before serving.

Don't Miss!

MAKES ABOUT 4 CUPS.

Raspberry Salsa

6 ounces fresh raspberries, rinsed
1 (11-ounce) can mandarin
    oranges, drained
1 teaspoon cinnamon
1 tablespoon light boysenberry
    syrup
Dash of Chambord (raspberry)
    liqueur (optional)

This combination of fresh and canned fruits makes a great topper for desserts.

Combine all ingredients in a medium bowl. Stir gently to combine. Chill for no more than 1 hour.

Stir and Serve

MAKES ABOUT 2 CUPS.

Border Jumper Salsa

Mark Lauffer likes to use this salsa with beef brisket and smoky beans. Lauffer's kitchen tip for salsa makers: Storing salsa in plastic can leave a lasting impression. Dedicate one special bowl to the salsa cause.

Combine lime juice, salt, pepper, and green chiles in a large bowl. Add remaining ingredients and stir. After the salsa rests for a while, liquid rises to the top; you may discard it or stir it back in.

Entertaining

MAKES ABOUT 5 CUPS.

1 tablespoon lime juice
Salt and pepper to taste
1 (7-ounce) can diced green chiles
1 (15-ounce) can whole tomatoes, drained, torn into small pieces
3 bunches thin green onions including tops, diced
1 large, firm tomato, diced
½ green bell pepper, diced
1 jalapeño, seeded and diced
¼ cup chopped cilantro
10 ounces of your favorite ready-made salsa

Fresh Orange Salsa

We both have backyard citrus trees, which means that sooner or later we put orange in everything. Orange Salsa is great with grilled chicken or shrimp.

Combine all ingredients gently in a medium bowl. Cover and chill for 30 minutes or more.

Versatile

MAKES ABOUT 2 CUPS.

2 oranges, peeled and diced
½ cup finely chopped red onion
2 tablespoons chopped cilantro or parsley
2 tablespoons lemon or lime juice
2 jalapeños, seeded and minced
1 clove garlic, minced

Pineapple Salsa

½ fresh pineapple, diced, or 1 (20-ounce) can pineapple chunks, diced
1 green apple, peeled and diced
1 jalapeño (or 2 serranos for more heat), seeded and minced
1 green onion, diced
2 tablespoons minced cilantro
2 tablespoons lime or lemon juice

Inspired by the pineapple salsa at Scottsdale's Mariott Mountain Shadows Resort, this is an intensely flavorful recipe. The resort serves it with Ahi tuna, which you can sear or grill.

Combine all ingredients in a medium bowl and chill for 30 minutes.

Stir and Serve

MAKES ABOUT 3 CUPS.

Mango and Roasted Corn Salsa

2 cups fresh corn kernels cut from the cob (about 3 ears) or 2 cups best-quality frozen corn, thawed
1 teaspoon vegetable oil
2 cups peeled, diced mango (about 2 mangoes)
¼ cup lemon or lime juice
3 tablespoons diced onion
2 tablespoons minced fresh mint
2 tablespoons chopped cilantro
1½ teaspoons grated fresh ginger
¼ teaspoon salt

Roasting corn brings out a whole new deep flavor, which melds perfectly with mango and herbs in this unusual salsa.

Preheat oven to 400 degrees. Toss corn with oil and spread evenly on a baking sheet. Bake for 15 minutes. Cool. Combine corn with remaining ingredients and gently toss.

Festive

MAKES ABOUT 4 CUPS.

Opposite (clockwise from upper left): Cowboy Caviar, page 54; Green Salsa with Cucumbers and Avocados, page 58; Fresh Orange Salsa, page 59; Raspberry Salsa, page 58.

Real Salsa

1 (15-ounce) can diced tomatoes
   or 2 large, ripe tomatoes,
   chopped
1 (4-ounce) can chopped green
   chiles or 3 Anaheim chiles,
   roasted, peeled, and diced
1 large onion, diced
1 jalapeño, finely minced (optional)
½ teaspoon oregano (optional)
¼ teaspoon cumin
1 tablespoon olive oil (optional)
Salt and pepper to taste

Exactly what it says! And yes, the oregano is authentic to classic salsa. The herb is widely used in Mexico, often in combination with cumin.

Combine all ingredients in a medium bowl. Serve at once, or chill.

Stir and Serve

MAKES ABOUT 2 CUPS.

Kathy's Salsa

1 (10-ounce) can tomatoes with
   green chiles and onions, such
   as Ro-tel brand
1½ jalapeños (or less to taste),
   chopped
½ cup chopped fresh cilantro
3 green onions, chopped
Chopped garlic to taste (optional)
Canned green chiles to taste
   (optional)
1 tablespoon fresh lime juice
½ teaspoon cumin
Salt and pepper to taste

Kathy Blake-Novotny shared this recipe and the secret of this salsa's success: It contains all the things she likes!

Place tomatoes, jalapeños, cilantro and onions (and garlic and green chiles if using) in a blender and chop (do not blend) for about two minutes. Or process—just until chopped—in a food processor fitted with the steel blade. Pour into a medium bowl. At this point, you can cover and chill the salsa to use later. Just before serving, add lime juice, cumin, salt, and pepper.

Festive

MAKES ABOUT 3 CUPS.

Roasted Pineapple-Carrot Salsa

You will love this! You can eat it with chips, serve it with pork tenderloin or ham, or use it our favorite way, in the Goat Cheese, Salsa, and Shrimp Nachos on page 15.

Preheat oven to 450 degrees. Place pineapple on a baking sheet or baking dish and brush with oil. Place in oven for 15 minutes. Add onion, brush with oil, and bake 10 more minutes. Add jalapeño, brush with oil, and bake 10 more minutes, or until all three are brown. Remove from oven and cool. Dice all three and combine with bell pepper in a large bowl.

Meanwhile, cook carrot in boiling water for 4 minutes or just until crisp-tender. Combine carrot with remaining ingredients. Add to pineapple mixture and stir well.

Make Ahead

MAKES ABOUT 3 CUPS.

1 (20-ounce) can pineapple chunks, drained (juice reserved)
1½ teaspoons hot sesame oil or dark sesame oil combined with ⅛ teaspoon red pepper flakes, ground
1 inch-thick slice red onion
1 jalapeño
¼ cup diced yellow or red bell pepper
½ cup chopped carrot
2 tablespoons lime juice
2 tablespoons pineapple juice
1 tablespoon cider vinegar
1 teaspoon brown sugar
1 teaspoon grated fresh ginger
⅛ teaspoon ground allspice

Mediterranean Olive Salsa

8 ounces Greek or Kalamata
    olives, pitted and chopped
1 large tomato, chopped
4 ounces feta cheese, crumbled
3 or 4 green onions, chopped
2 tablespoons olive oil (or less)
2 tablespoons white wine vinegar

This tangy olive relish is great on pita or bagel chips, and it's also wonderful sprinkled over greens to make an instant Greek salad. Or spread it on submarine sandwich buns with cold cuts and a little oregano.

Combine all ingredients in a medium bowl. Serve at room temperature. Chill for storage.

Versatile

MAKES ABOUT 2½ CUPS.

Salsa with Avocado

½ onion, chopped
1 large red tomato, diced
2 small avocados, peeled and
    diced
½ teaspoon chopped garlic
2 dried chile pequins or chile
    tepíns, crushed
1 teaspoon lime juice
3 shakes powdered cumin
3 shakes powdered cayenne
1 teaspoon Durkee's Hot Sauce

Avocados can be used in salsa as well as guacamole. They give this salsa, a favorite of Judy's son Mack, a velvety texture.

Combine all ingredients in a small bowl and chill. Serve promptly.

Traditional

MAKES ABOUT 2 CUPS.

Los Conchas Tomatillo Salsa

Fresh tomatillos are available more widely than ever. When you find them in your produce department, take them home and make your family or friends happy with this salsa. Remove the papery husks of fresh tomatillos and wash them well under warm water. They will feel almost soapy.

Place tomatillos in a medium bowl. Cover and microwave 3 minutes on high, stirring halfway through cooking.

Combine tomatillos and fresh chiles in food processor or blender. Chop roughly by pulsing. Do not overprocess. Add cilantro. Pulse briefly again. Turn into medium bowl and stir in remaining ingredients.

Cover and refrigerate. Let flavors meld at least 2 hours before serving.

Have on Hand

MAKES ABOUT 3 CUPS.

1 pound fresh tomatillos, stemmed and roughly chopped, or 1 (15- or 16-ounce) can tomatillos, drained
2 fresh green chiles, such as 1 jalapeño and 1 Anaheim, seeded
½ bunch cilantro, stems removed
1 (4-ounce) can chopped green chiles
Juice of 1 lime
1 tablespoon honey
1 tablespoon olive oil
Salt to taste

Mack's Hot Sauce

½ cup de-stemmed, small hot
    peppers
¼ cup apple cider vinegar
1 clove garlic

*Mack Walker loves hot sauce with his breakfast burritos.
He makes hot sauce with black chiltepin peppers growing in
the backyard, but you can use any kind of small, fresh,
hot pepper, such as the tiny red and green Christmas
peppers common around the holidays.*

Put all ingredients in food processor and purée. Decant into
a bottle and store in refrigerator. Use sparingly! It's very hot.
Use within two weeks.

Muy Picante

MAKES ABOUT ½ CUP.

Joy's Salsa

6 jalapeños, stemmed, seeded,
    and coarsely chopped
2 Anaheim chiles, stemmed,
    seeded, and coarsely chopped
2 (28-ounce) cans crushed
    tomatoes
½ large white onion, chopped
¼ to ½ cup chopped cilantro
2 green onions
1 tablespoon chopped garlic
½ tablespoon fresh oregano
1 tablespoon salt
½ tablespoon pepper

*No, this salsa is not named for its emotional effect,
although it will make you happy! It is named for creator
Joy Lambert.*

Place all ingredients in a blender or food processor and whir
or pulse to desired consistency. Remove to a large bowl and
chill at least 3 hours.

Muy Picante

MAKES ABOUT 6 CUPS.

INDEX